CORRUPTION:
WRAPPING PUBLIC AUTHORITY
FOR THE SAKE OF OWN
PERSONAL SELF

A Personal & Private Journalism

Experience

BY

DR. AHMAD MARDINI

aberdeen university
press services

Printed in the United States of America
ISBN: 978-0-578-01671-9

This book is printed on 6" x 9", perfect binding, 60# cream interior paper, black and white interior ink, 100# white exterior paper, full-color exterior ink. Prices are subject to change.

Cover Title Designed by Aberdeen University Press Services.

CORRUPTION: WRAPPING PUBLIC AUTHORITY FOR THE SAKE

OF OWN PERSONAL SELF

First Edition

Ahmad Mardini

"All corruption fighters who are shielded by Science and Virginity. And to all Survivals from the disease of time and place. I grant this experiment... With all possible effort."

- Dr. Ahmad Mardini

TABLE OF CONTENTS

INTRODUCTION

Social and development scientists see that morals form a "productive investment", so through that statement, the national forces always work for fighting corruption that stand behind any destruction for development's operations)) Accordingly we had this vision in Syria, and have had seen this in the past Syrian president and the new one as well through their Articles and speeches in parliament.

As journalist in "Teshreen Newspaper" (Department of Investigation).It was honored for me to practice that role with my colleagues ,therefore I had lots of statements articles taking the economical and manage mental, and developmental side in great consideration, documented and proof, which gave me the acceptable results This research and study was been held on my long and personal experiment in that field "corruption", its cause and form besides its results and proper methods to put it away nationally and internationally Taking in consideration some of the samples Due to corruption cases published in many   Arabic and global newspapers with suggestions for fixing this disease, managementally and economically as possible as.

SECTION - I

SOME IDEAS OF CORRUPTION

Social scientists who involved in third world problems, especially Asia, have got that results as long as good management in their official departments as long as brides are less, besides their economy has high grown up gradually with time.

Studying corruption phenomena started many years ago, and lots of researches refer it to moral behave affecting negatively on economics of countries, where some say that corruption may increase the validity and performance the nation's economy in rare cases.

Which leads us to two kinds of corruptions:

1. Corruption increase the affection of economy cycle.
2. Corruption decreases the affection of economy cycle.

Ahmad Mardini © 2009

Through this confused result vision some could increase the economical value, when find a way to not apply the non effective official laws that prevent more effective performance.

For instance, paying brides by farmers to the administrative system in China let the seeds transfer between counties easier than usual governmental methods which lead to much more seeds production.

Besides, some economics believe that corruption is less harmful" for economics if it was organized and expectable.

In some countries many big effective companies, have brides budget to organize and facility its procedures.

With all what mentioned above regarding corruption, still its negative effects more than its positive relying on:

1. Paid bride will be in service budget's account and goods, and this will negatively affect on consumer and tax payments.

Ahmad Mardini © 2009

2. The week producers who pay prides will get bigger share than effective ones Investors trust will be much less by existing laws and rules, and let them feel More risky taking in consideration the economical interest.

3. Confusion occurred due to the non specific brides takers.

4. Big bride's givers prevent new coming to the market

Most economists' analysis besides international bankers' specialists say that just in rare cases "corruption might be positive"

In general as long as the country is rich and developed the corruption's percentage is less.

Although the link between corruption and income is mutual, not causative, we can deduce the following:

The economical mechanism and the laws leading it is a real law for developing and its presence forms an obstacle for the positive results created by the studied open economics followed by the laws and rules that already mentioned which include the roots of corruption and create the motives for individuals to break it.

There are another reason to the increasing of corruption which is the governmental weak ness and the more routine and bureaucratic.

As a wiser Indian said "if the king want to know if part of his money is stolen its difficulty is as your knowledge, if the fish drinks from the river it swims in!"

One of the most important points of view about corruption is the one related to Dr. Salah Wazzan [1] who wrote about corruption in his book (Arabic Agriculture Development) chapter twelve saying that this phenomenon is not a special sickness or shame due to only south. North is not empty of corruption as well.

But there are fundamental differences between the two cases, corruption in north is limited and its affection on national economic and rejected by their individuals and seriously tracked legally by law. On condition that is inside the country where inside the border, especially if it is related by

---

[1] Dr. Salah Wazzan is a Syrian from Latakia, specialist and consultant in UFO and UN

southern countries all will be converted and standards.

So corruption become in many cases mean for commercial advertisement.

Corruption increased lately in many Arabic countries and became like octopus wraps most of political and influence people.

SECTION - II

CORRUPTION MECHANISM
AND
IT'S RESULTS

Corruption has its own mechanism, which usually mix between what is public and what is private .so a new system been created called Farm Country, on other side it is like monster, so that for stealing $1 the corruptor won't dare spending $ 1000 in faked projects and fields not necessary for any, just for having his own commission.

Lost here is enlarged and its cost will go to the national income negatively.

Corruption affects on job's value as it is one of the most valuable value in healthy society which leads to the a miserable and laziness to the worker and producers and makes demonstrations so heavy and slow in productions.

Some say that corruption plays the role of" keep wheels oily" keeping in mind that the great mean merchants and economists in Arabic world did not go up to the productive corruption yet Besides corruption affects in the value of the work as one of the honest valuable ……

By canceling that value or dropping it down due to the wild nature and breaking its production.

For substituting the drop of purchasing value to the bride's employees salaries, it is also harmful through its final complication gives spreading out in the nation gives the non confidence between citizens and governments which leads the developed countries to cut the financial funds to those corrupted countries.

A study for the "International Funds Safe" about eight countries from the 3rd world gave that the Ratio of smuggled money to the total debts money is 30% which means that each one dollar get in to those countries as a loan a 30 cents passed the boarders at the same moment outside this country.

SECTION - III

THE DISTRIBUTING OF CORRUPTION AND THE MISSING INCHARGE (RESPONSIBLE)

There is a possibility for those regimes in the top responsible factors either positive or negative and could be added to some; such as Gas, petroleum and oil1`s fortune in some Arabic countries and starting the policy of corruption with western countries besides the Non Governmental big firms and companies.

Therefore, the political and economical sociable level for citizens will be non covalent with European states.

On addition to this discussing, relation between corrupted politicians with their families will form an octopus running the country from its west to east,

Working on controlling and denominate the financial resources where the commissions and others went into   pocket where the rest surely won't go for the best.

It is very important to remind that industrial countries play a bad role in the cooperation and protecting this Mop in south.

So, this European financial support is the secret weapon through economical competition was to invite the poor markets, which form its denomination on the continuity of such countries Struggling against corruption could not by the methods of morality or by using conscious .

This fighting could require a general population support and official ones as well, exactly as struggling against diseases, where, as some procedures will be mentioned in two terms.

1. Taking conscience's people to the highest possible degree and reconsider the social values and morals and relying on efficiency and trust.
2. Supporting the courts and law without any exceptions.

Ahmad Mardini © 2009

SECTION - IV

SO WHAT IS OUR ROLE HERE?

All what stated before was in general, in the 3rd world including Arab world.

We special trial with corruption in Syria because this party ruling that country.

The contradiction and mutual relations between politicians-government and the ruled party (Baath Party)[2] principle lead to a huge corruption that leads to the slowing of growing in Syria and to their low national income for the Syrian citizen.

Before answering any questions I would like to notify that those corruptors who are shielded by money and power became an effective grouping parliamentarian and responsible for the laws in the country exposing Tax on food, cars, restaurants etc. on citizens dealing pretending that this is luxury tax have to be paid.

---

[2] Baath party is the Syrian ruler party in Syria since 1970

For history, the past Syrian president, had questioned the government then. and let many ministries resigned and went in to judgment in 1993.

In an interview with French T.V, the past Syrian president mentioned the ways of corruption's fighting by him on 11/03/1999.
But this couldn't be happened and a new
government been formed from the powerful man's sons which lead the corruption in that country to be organized and public working along all the departments ministries, so the new government been changed again and a new one has been formed by Dr,Mouhammad Mostafa Miroon[3] on 07/03/2000 without any effect.

Now there is another government whose its Prime Minister is "Muhammad Naji Al-Uttri" that put plans to struggle that octopus ,hope success.

---

[3] Formal Syrian Prime Minister

SECTION – V

THE CORRUPTION OF PRIVATE SECTIONS: IS THAT REAL DANGEROUS

Not corruption is only linked to official department but even to the private establishment as well, which stand basically behind.

Most of the corruption's cases in government's systems, though bribing the official Employees whatever their position is.

Businessmen, merchants, industrialists, etc. have relation linkage between the responsible ones in governments by marriage or by way or another.

So you see lots of virtual projects and using public banks through having big unreal loans.

Besides, the virtual export for the sake of getting the dollar's privilege exportation and dealing with it in the black market besides their importing to the materials that remanufactured and export it to other nations in the purpose of factories working and not selling it in the Syrian markets because it is not included in taxes and custom's fees.

Although the selling of that manufacture's materials going to be sold by smuggling it in Partnership with custom's men with Aleppo's merchants, and lots of other methods which lead by force to lead to the official employee in most sections to be corrupted.

SECTION – VI

JOURNALISM'S ROLE

The role of journalism was important in fighting corruption especially since 1970,but Its dare role started in the earlier nineties and Its peak was in 1996 until 2000 where the journalism took much interested from the past Syrian president and the present one as well, so many corruption files opened and I was honored to be investigate in many files which I personally published some of them in the public newspaper "Teshreen[4]" and through this experiment we could maintain some common points.

Here are some:

Some samples of corruption cases in Syria published by Syrian newspapers:

---

[4] "Tesheren" is a government news paper authorized by the ruling Party in Syria

1. THE ASSOCAITION OF FARMERS IN "AIN AL ARAB" would be a sample for the association threatened by broke.

2. The manager of the association and encounter stole 11.5 million S.P as well as the association's bankers were accused too.

3. "Reservation of the stealer properties"

TESHREEN NEWSPAPER/PAGE 4; ON 18-01-1997.

SECTION - VII

"HOW TO MINIMZE CORRUPTION"

THE CONTROLLING OF MANAGEMENT FIRST OR ECONOMICAL ONES?

After all what represented and to get rid of corruption,

Do we have to start 1st with controlling management or economical ones.

Most researches get though this question looking for the best answer, as both are linked by way or another in economical, sociable and political and even managing.

And its been identified by the " **International Monetary Fund**": It is wrapping to the general public power for the **SAKE OF PRIVATE ECONOMICAL SECTIONS**.

Regarding to what mentioned corruption spread out through our entire world and it is going to be wider.

Therefore, what is the solution then? Is it economical, political as INTERNATIONAL organizations state or through management first? By putting rules for the development cycle instead of its role is protecting and guarding its mistakes and his money.

SECTION - VIII

"CONTROLLING MANAGEMENT"
-an introduction

This phenomena in its spreading more and more in our societies, we see that controlling and fixing the managements which will be the basics in government for running fixed programs economical programs and developed ones running fixed programs economics and developed ones were interested by scientists and researchers and held many public committees which in Syria was Tuesday's community, where many discussions and decisions which gave after lots of conferences every Tuesday the following summary:

1. The spreading of management corruption and the interference of its mechanisms.

The facts are the corruptive cases in financial and management during the past years in Syria, where a report been handed by the chief of financial controlling stating that 2253 main establishment in both sections; economical and managing and 787 branched establishments in 1998 have taken lots of corruptive cases which deeply gives the feeling of the importance to relieve the damages coming because of corruption that holds and protect this octopus, using a new and productive methods to get rid from it.

2. The enlargement of the country's expenses and the increasing of governmental system against weakness of services and resources whose pretending fighting corruption.

3. Communication and information's` revolution and what reflect from canceling to the walls and borders regarding knowledge taking and giving. This urged going to develop and having the wish to get any modern idea whereas come.

4. Inquiring international foundations and regional organizations that offer loan and assistants to do radical controlling the management system. so as have the capacity to understand all what modern in investments the assistants for The sake of government.

From all what we mentioned we conclude;

That we should have a clear strategy for fighting corruption not just talking and making or holding conferences for dealing this problem without putting a strategy held by good people that may run it. So, many questions now are in mind that lead us to:

Studying the basis of our traditional habits, values, etc for our society to build a successful strategy.

1. Build mental route for fixing management held on development from inside the Syrian society relying on seizing its positive basis form all what modern cultures to obtain a better fact.

2. Not passing the idea of controlling management, as an artistic and abstract operation.

So that develops the frames and gets the organized sections.

3. The assurance of continuity of efforts regarding management controlling(fixing) and dealing as workshop and future plan to treat different negative phenomena's that been formed, and which could form a bright future .

4. Offering the first; care; to the human beings along the rest of management treating in Syria considering the goal of fixing and its mean for starting specialized statistics which saves precise statistics and the clear data for the present and future needs in market, and determine its needs and which could offer by training and teaching and clarify the places of needs.

5. Achieve equilibrium in getting technical substances for management control in Syria.

6. Supporting and motivating management control effort in POLITICAL LEADERSHIP in Syria.

7. Obtaining public and citizens agreement according to the fact through declaration to the expectable results due to the plan put by government and not to be over reacted using tools for sudden change, so the fixing management gains its honest towards work not p

8. List the controlling for management's plan schedule.

9. The consultants and managers should collect the possible qualified people so it might be a stream to afford its idea and share through their suggestions.

10. Collecting efforts for the public voice to wrap around the controlling of management in Syria.

SECTION - IX

ECONOMICAL CONTROL

AND

CORRUPTION FIGHTING

And what about the economical arrangement regarding corruption's fighting?

- The more convincing, is about fixing economical management, that leads to avoid as much as possible corruptions` factors and working to give the chances, opportunities for working class and medium one, that may limit the illegal getting rich or the money that should go to the government will shift out these countries because of corruption. so we believe that there are three procedures to decrease it:

    1. The availability of political background to oppose it.

Ahmad Mardini © 2009

2. The clarity of mentality system in economics.

3. Existing of the organized environment.

Experiments lead us to the fault of that system (management control space time without limit), because economical fixing must be a mean to managing orders from one side and seizing production on the other side.

So, there must the following goals be available for controlling program.

1- Managing the whole order and achieving equilibrium in whole economics as well. As swallowing enlargement is the important one.

2- Charging whole materialisms and humanities to serve the development operation.

3- Increasing the efficiency in economical role and in distributing resources.

Ahmad Mardini © 2009

4- Creating the seizing atmosphere for long time investment, and finding all available opportunities for all as could as possible.

5- Increasing the investments` profit through releasing the obstacles and stabilities in environment.

6- Encouraging the direct foreign investments with directing this investments through the primary local development according to financial encouraging

7- Stop imperialism in and let the competition deep in market.

8- Trying to keep our young educated people to stay home to share the country in building it, through giving them the suitable atmosphere.

SECTION - X

THE FUTURE GOVERNMENT`S PROJECTS

In 2002 the government hold a wide and positive plan for controlling plan, but unfortunately for unknown reasons that plan went to donor, where a new management controlling instead appear.

So here we stand along lots questions such as:

Is the management controlling must be the basic one? And is it necessary to have two separated plans for fixing and erasing corruption?

So lots of questions, wherever Syria could stand economical pressure and kept it's independent political and economical ones, all because its independent decision.

Therefore the required control must be through general development.

Finally;

The challenging coming inside and outside that Syria facing now is huge and so complicated where all those challenges increased because we were slow in fixing management controlling and economical one, using different excuses, so we have now get started and to face those challenges, and go through fixing and controlling taking its general concept followed with economical development and humanities ones besides technological.

APPENDIX - I

REFERENCES & BIBLIOGRAPHY

*Our Strategically Choice
Dr.Bashar Al Asad, Edited by Dr.Rima Jamous and Imad Al Karaky.
Published by: National Information Center /July 2000

*Eng.Ayman Abd AlNour (Al Moharrer News); Issue #2471.

*The Arabic Nation Isuue #1218 on 7/7/2000

*Dr.Nabil Sukkar- Economical Control in Syria – (Lecturer Notes)

*Dr.Dial Al Haj Aref. Management Fixing in Syria – (Lecturer Notes)

*Ahmad Abdul Sallam Dabbas -The Management Fixing as an Introduction to Economical Control (Lecturer Notes)

*Collections of Journalist's articles on Teshreen Newspaper.

Index

APPENDIX - II

ABOUT AUTHOR

Dr. Ahmad Sharif Mardini was born in Syria in 1956. He holds B.S in Geography, from Damascus University, Syria.

He is editor in Al-Teshreen and Al-Thawra News since 1982 till date. He is also Editor, Investigation Department at Al-Teshreen Newspaper.

Dr. Ahmad is also author of "Al Hasake Hohafaza". His is also serving as General Coordinator for the International Scientists Foundation in Syria and Lebanon, based in Alexandria / Egypt.

He is also General-Assistant Arabic European Center in Syria, based in Germany.

Since 1998, Dr. Ahmad is also working as General Manager at Union Associations Cooperative for Living" in Damascus.

NOTES